THIS BOOK BELONGS TO

_____

FOR THE KIDS WHO SECRETLY
WANT TO BECOME A NINJA

ISBN: 9798894581835

IN THE QUIET HILLS OF WINDSHADOW VALLEY
STOOD A SECRET DOJO,
HIDDEN AMONG THE TREES.
THIS WAS NO ORDINARY DOJO.
IT TRAINED THE FIERCEST NINJAS.

INSIDE, RIKU, A SMALL BOY WITH BIG DREAMS,
CLUTCHED HIS WOODEN PRACTICE SWORD.
HIS HANDS WERE SWEATY. HIS KNEES SHOOK.

"FOCUS, RIKU!" MASTER KEN BARKED.
"A NINJA MUST BE SWIFT AND PRECISE!"

RIKU NODDED, THEN TRIPPED OVER HIS OWN FEET.
HIS CLASSMATES, ESPECIALLY HIRO, THE TOP STUDENT, BURST INTO LAUGHTER.

"YOU'LL NEVER BE A REAL NINJA," HIRO SNEERED. "YOU'RE TOO CLUMSY!"

RIKU'S CHEEKS BURNED, BUT HE CLENCHED HIS FISTS.
"I'LL SHOW THEM," HE WHISPERED.

THAT NIGHT, RIKU PRACTICED IN THE MOONLIT COURTYARD.
HE BALANCED ON THIN ROPES, FLIPPED OVER BARRELS,
AND SWUNG HIS SWORD. BUT HE STILL STUMBLED AND FELL.

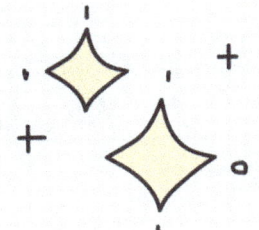

THE NEXT MORNING, MASTER KEN ANNOUNCED, "TOMORROW IS THE SHADOW CHALLENGE. ONLY THE WORTHY CAN STAY IN THIS DOJO."

HIRO SMIRKED AT RIKU. "YOU MIGHT AS WELL PACK YOUR BAGS."

RIKU IGNORED HIM, FOCUSING ON THE ANNOUNCEMENT.
THE SHADOW CHALLENGE? WHAT WAS IT?

THAT NIGHT, RIKU CREPT INTO THE LIBRARY.
HE FOUND AN OLD SCROLL ABOUT THE SHADOW CHALLENGE.
IT SPOKE OF TESTS IN SPEED, STEALTH, AND STRATEGY.

AS HE READ, RIKU HAD AN IDEA.
HE WOULDN'T OUTFIGHT HIRO—HE'D OUTSMART HIM.

THE NEXT DAY, THE STUDENTS GATHERED IN THE MISTY FOREST.
MASTER KEN EXPLAINED, "RETRIEVE THE GOLDEN BELL FROM THE MOUNTAINTOP
AND RETURN UNSEEN. USE YOUR SKILLS WISELY."

THE STUDENTS DASHED INTO THE FOREST, DISAPPEARING INTO THE SHADOWS.
RIKU TOOK A DEEP BREATH AND FOLLOWED.

HIRO SPRINTED AHEAD, LEAPING FROM TREE TO TREE.
HE WAS FAST, BUT HE DIDN'T NOTICE THE SNAPPING TWIGS UNDERFOOT.

RIKU MOVED SLOWER BUT QUIETER, CAREFULLY STUDYING THE FOREST.
HE NOTICED TRAPS: A NET HIDDEN UNDER LEAVES, A TRIPWIRE NEAR THE PATH.

USING A STICK, RIKU TRIGGERED THE TRAPS BEFORE THEY COULD CATCH HIM.
HE GRINNED. "THINK, DON'T RUSH," HE TOLD HIMSELF.

AHEAD, HIRO REACHED THE MOUNTAIN BUT SLIPPED ON LOOSE ROCKS.
"CLUMSY FOOL," HE MUTTERED, UNAWARE RIKU WAS WATCHING.

RIKU CLIMBED SLOWLY, SPOTTING HANDHOLDS HIRO MISSED.
THE GOLDEN BELL GLEAMED AT THE TOP.

HIRO LUNGED FOR IT BUT STUMBLED AGAIN, KNOCKING THE BELL LOOSE.
IT ROLLED DOWN THE MOUNTAIN.

RIKU DARTED AFTER THE BELL, HIS SMALL SIZE HELPING HIM SLIP THROUGH TIGHT SPACES. HE CAUGHT IT JUST BEFORE IT HIT A RAVINE.

BUT NOW, HIRO WAS BLOCKING THE PATH. "GIVE ME THE BELL," HE DEMANDED.

RIKU SHOOK HIS HEAD. "A NINJA DOESN'T STEAL. THEY EARN."

HIRO LUNGED, BUT RIKU SIDESTEPPED, USING HIS CLUMSINESS TO DODGE HIRO'S ATTACK. HIRO TRIPPED ON A ROOT AND FELL INTO A MUDDY PUDDLE.

RIKU TOOK OFF, CAREFULLY AVOIDING NOISY PATHS AND STICKING TO SHADOWS.
HE COULD HEAR HIRO STOMPING AND GROWLING BEHIND HIM.

AT LAST, RIKU REACHED THE DOJO. HE RANG THE GOLDEN BELL,
ITS CHIME ECHOING THROUGH THE VALLEY.

THE STUDENTS EMERGED FROM THE FOREST, HIRO AMONG THEM, COVERED IN MUD.
MASTER KEN SMILED.

"RIKU HAS PROVEN THAT A NINJA'S GREATEST WEAPON IS THEIR MIND," MASTER KEN DECLARED.

RIKU COULDN'T BELIEVE IT. "I BELONG HERE,"
HE WHISPERED, HIS CHEST SWELLING WITH PRIDE.

HIRO SCOWLED BUT SAID NOTHING. DEEP DOWN, HE KNEW RIKU HAD EARNED IT.

FROM THAT DAY ON, RIKU TRAINED HARDER THAN EVER, KNOWING EVEN CLUMSY NINJAS COULD RISE TO GREATNESS.

AND IN THE SECRET DOJO OF WINDSHADOW VALLEY, RIKU'S NAME BECAME A LEGEND, PROVING THAT STRENGTH WASN'T JUST IN THE BODY—IT WAS IN THE HEART AND MIND.

THE END

BE SURE TO CHECK OUT OUR SERIES AND BUY BOOK 2 OF THIS SERIES
RIKU THE CLUMSY NINJA